THE GALS & GUYS FROM

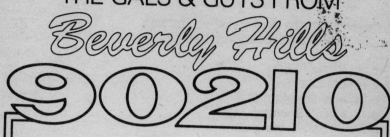

Beverly Hills 90210

By
Sara James

kidsbooks
Incorporated

Copyright © 1992 Kidsbooks, Inc.
7004 N. California Avenue
Chicago, IL 60645

ISBN: 1-56156-137-1

Manufactured in the United States of America

TABLE OF CONTENTS

INTRODUCTION

Is *90210* your favorite show? Do you get your thrills from the *Hills*? Is your special star the coolest by far? If you answered yes to these questions, no doubt you're glued to the tube every week for another episode of the *Beverly Hills, 90210*!

From the start this show had the potential to be big...really big. It had all the ingredients: cool teenagers; happening Beverly Hills; superstar producer Aaron Spelling; top-notch writers; and most importantly a very talented cast!

But what really draws you to this show? Is it the realistic, up-to-date issues that are explored on the show? Is it characters that you can relate to? Or is it the talented ensemble of actors? Most likely it's a combination of all of them, but the fact that the actors and actresses are so good-looking doesn't hurt!

In this book you can satisfy all your *90210* cravings. There's up-to-the-minute, behind the scenes *Beverly Hills* gossip, quotable quotes from you know who, and of course a sneak peak into the real lives of the *90210* cast. But if that's not enough, you can get hip to the zip with the *Beverly Hills, 90210* Trivia Quiz and personalized puzzles from each of the stars. Read on!

Jason Priestley does the talk show scene.

CHAPTER 1

Jason Priestley Plays Brandon Walsh

Many people become actors because they want to live in a world with chauffeured limousines, star-studded parties, and adoring fans. But Jason Priestley became an actor because he just plain loves to act. This Canadian-bred guy has had dreams of being an actor from the time he was a toddler, and while he's determined to make a name for himself, he's also determined to maintain his private life.

Jay was born on August 28, 1969 to Lorne and Sharon Priestley in Vancouver, British Columbia, Canada. He launched his acting career at the tender age of five years and his first role was in a TV movie called *Stacey*. Jason did not go unnoticed—how could anyone miss those baby blues—and soon became a busy child actor. He did Canadian commercials, theater, and movies until he reached high school.

As a teenager, Jason wanted to spread his

wings and fly away from acting for a bit. "I wanted to be a kid, and I was a kid," explains Jason who went through a punk period in high school. When looking back at this time, Jason calls himself, "a rebel without a clue."

However, Jason knew enough to recognize that acting was in his blood and after high school he once again returned to the screen. Although Jason landed some American roles while still living in Canada, guest-starring on *MacGyver*, *Danger Bay*, and *21 Jump Street*, he realized that staying in Vancouver would limit his roles. So he headed out to Hollywood, land of the rich and famous, and where every young actor hopes his dreams will come true.

For Jason the story does have a happy ending. Once settled in LA, Jay quickly landed roles in the Disney flicks *Teen Angel* and *Teen Angel Returns*. Then, in 1989, Jason starred in the short-lived sitcom *Sister Kate*. It was on that show that Tori Spelling first set eyes on Jason and told her producer father, Aaron, that he was perfect for the part of Brandon. And perfect Jay was.

Jason fell right in with the rest of the *90210* ensemble, and liked the show immediately. While Jason claims he and Brandon are very different, he thinks Brandon is a good character to play. "He's a nice guy, but not too perfect." Jason is now considered the show's quarterback and from the looks of things he's making a lot of touchdowns.

Off the set, Jason is a winner, too. While he still maintains his privacy, he does step into the spotlight for fund-raisers and promotional tours. He plays on a Sunday morning celebrity hockey team, whose proceeds go to charity. Jay is also involved in raising money for the Starlight Foundation. Recently, he and the rest of the *90210* gang accepted an award for their fund-raising efforts. When it came time for the Jaybird to make a speech, he could hardly get the words out, he was so choked up!

For now, Jason is very happy with the way his life is going. As to what's next, he'll hopefully star in some movies and of course, lots more *Beverly Hills, 90210!*

**Shannen Doherty is the beautiful
brunette who plays Brenda Walsh.**

CHAPTER 2

Shannen Doherty Plays Brenda Walsh

While Brenda Walsh is very concerned about "fitting in" with the cool crowd, Shannen Doherty is much more independent and always has been!

Born April 12, 1971 in Memphis, Tennessee, Shannen and her family moved to Los Angeles when she was just six. Two years later Shannen went with a friend on a local audition and decided right then and there that she wanted to be an actress. Although her parents thought eight was a little young for such a big decision, Shannen was determined. Within two years she proved to her folks that she could act in local theater, keep up with her schoolwork, and maintain a "normal" life. What's a parent to do?

Tom and Rosa Doherty gave in to their strong-willed little girl and soon Shannen was acting on TV. She guest-starred on *Father Murphy* which led to a starring part in the series *Little House: A New Beginning.* Soon after that, Shannen landed the leading role of Kris Witherspoon in the long-running drama *Our House.*

When *Our House* was canceled, Shannen had parts in the movies *Heathers, Night Shift,* and *Girls Just Want to Have Fun,* among others. And then of course came you know what. Shannen was thrilled to land one of the starring roles in *Beverly Hills, 90210* and couldn't be more pleased with her character, Brenda Walsh. Shannen feels that she's helping Brenda grow more independent, and that she's sending positive messages out to the show's audience.

"We all get to have a lot of input into the show. So if there's something Brenda does or says that I'm not comfortable with, I can say so. And that gives me a way to send messages to the fans. For example, there were scripts that had Brenda suggesting that she needed to lose weight—and I am like one of the skinniest people. Then I was getting letters from girls saying, 'If you need to lose weight, then I really must need to lose weight.' That scared me. I really thought we were sending out the wrong message. So I went to the producer and told him how I felt, and that was it. It was instantly written out."

One of the things Shannen does not want written out, however, is her free time off the set.

Shannen is a private person, and while she does enjoy shopping with best pal Tori Spelling, she also enjoys horseback riding, tennis, skiing, and exercising. She lives alone in a condo with her three dogs and three doves. Shannen is an animal lover and supports many animal shelters.

Most nights Shannen spends a quiet evening with close friends, or home alone reading and studying her lines. Shannen does however travel frequently...to Chicago that is. This beautiful brunette is seeing steady beau, 25-year-old Chris Foufas, a real estate developer from the windy city. Shannen thinks he's the perfect guy.

It seems as if Shannen's life is pretty perfect all around. When she looks to the future, she wants to continue acting, but feels family is very important. She says she wants to have five children. Hey Chris, has Shannen told you this yet?

Hunky Luke Perry portrays the incredibly popular Dylan McKay.

CHAPTER 3

Luke Perry plays Dylan McKay

No one famous ever came from Fredericktown, Ohio...until now that is! Coy Luther Perry III, while born on October 11, 1966 in Mansfield, Ohio, grew up in the small farming town of Fredericktown. He lived there with his mom Ann, stepfather Steve, brother Tom, sister Amy, and stepsister Emily.

At the early age of four, Luke knew he wanted to be an actor. One night his mom was watching the movie *Cool Hand Luke* with Paul Newman. Little Luke recognized his own name and was fascinated. He knew then that one day he would be on screen, too.

However, Fredericktown is not exactly the place one launches an acting career. It is rather the place where one works in the fields or in construction. There wasn't even a movie theater in Fredericktown, let alone a school drama club.

But Luke continued to dream and after high school, he began to make his dream a reality. Like Jason Priestley, Luke set out for Hollywood. But Tinseltown wasn't as kind to Luke as it was to Jason and roles never came his way. After three years, Luke decided to try New York City. It was there that he landed the role of Ned Bates on the afternoon soap opera *Loving*. But when Luke's *Loving* contract ran out, he decided to try Hollywood again.

This time, he was much luckier, and that's an understatement! Luke landed the role of Dylan McKay almost as soon as he arrived back in LA. Now his life is very different from the one he once led in Fredericktown. Come share a day with Luke and find out more about this really nice guy— who also happens to be gorgeous.

Luke gets up at all different times in the morning depending on what time he's due at the set. In TV talk that's known as his "call" time. First thing he does is feed his pet pig Jerry Lee, you know pigs are always hungry! However, lean Luke doesn't always have time for breakfast himself and often just dashes out the door.

Luke zooms off to the set on his motorcycle. He always wears a helmet, and looks forward to greeting his co-workers and friends. Affectionate Luke starts the day with hugs and kisses all around—hugs for the guys, that is—and kisses for the gals. Then Luke's off to makeup, as if he'd need any, and then to costume. Now Luke's ready to start his scenes.

This serious guy uses the method technique in acting. That means he calls up all his emotions to use in a scene. If Dylan has to be sad, Luke will think of painful things that happened to him in his past in order to convey that emotion. But when the director calls, "it's a wrap," and it's time for lunch, Luke bounces back to his jolly, warm self once again!

Lunch is one of Luke's favorite parts of the day. Besides the fact that he's usually starving because he probably skipped breakfast, Luke enjoys the time to hang out with his friends. "My friends are the most valuable things in my life," says Luke, and as you probably know the *90210* cast is real tight. But, Luke is still a businessman, and must use some of his lunchtime to make calls to his agent and family, and to read fan mail.

After lunch it's back to work. Luke throws himself right into his role again, until the director says, "it's a day." Depending on what time it is, Luke might hang out with best pals Jay and Ian, or go home for a quiet evening with Jerry Lee. Luke isn't into the Hollywood social scene—he likes his time alone to read, think, or watch old movies. Luke doesn't have a steady girl right now, but you can be sure he'll make time for one when she comes along.

But for now, Luke's content with the way things are going, and at the end of a long day, he sinks happily into bed, Jerry Lee at his side!

Gabrielle Carteris likes to invite
her castmates over for a homecooked meal.

CHAPTER 4

Gabrielle Carteris
Plays Andrea Zuckerman

Gabby's childhood dream was to be a famous ballerina. While she did study and perform with the San Francisco Ballet as a child, she had to eventually abandon her dream. She was simply too short. While this was a huge disappointment to Gabrielle, she switched gears and focused her energy on pantomime and acting. Aren't her fans today lucky she did!

Perky, petite Gabrielle Carteris was born on January 2nd in Arizona but moved with her mom and twin brother to San Francisco soon afterward. Gabby was a bright, bouncy, and curious child and also a terrific student. Although her outstanding academics would have made Andrea Zuckerman proud, Gabby also had many outside interests. Besides dance, Gabrielle was very interested in mime. She became so accomplished at it that at the age of 14 she was invited to join a troupe of professional mimes to tour Europe for the summer. "We went to Italy, France, Germany, and Austria and performed in the streets," remembers Gabrielle.

After graduating high school, Gabby wanted to pursue her acting career, but knew it was just as important to complete her education. She decided to attend Sarah Lawrence College in Westchester, N.Y. because it was a good school and was also close enough to New York City where she could attend auditions.

While roles did not fall at Gabby's feet, she was one determined gal and kept plugging away. Eventually she landed roles on After-School Specials and in the soap opera *Another World*. Gabby even spent her junior year in college studying with the Royal Academy of Dramatic arts in London so she could fine-tune her acting skills. Way to go, Gabby!

After college Gabrielle lived in New York City where she first crossed paths with Ian Ziering and Luke Perry. In 1990, she moved out to Tinseltown and made the rounds of auditions. One of those auditions just happened to be for a show called *Class of Beverly Hills*. That's what *90210* was initially called. Interestingly, Gabby originally tried out for the role of Brenda thinking that her real-life experience as a twin would help her in the part. While she didn't get that, she did win the role of bright and cute Andrea Zuckerman. "I totally love this character," says Gabrielle of Andrea. "I love that she is smart and beautiful."

Andrea is glad that her character is often the conscious voice of the show. She is glad to be sending positive messages out to teenagers. When asked what advice she would give teens who are going through a tough time Gabrielle says, "Make sure you talk to your friends. And family. Do not shut your family out. Love yourself. It will be okay. Life is about cycles, I think. Everytime there is a hard time, an easier time will come. Even though it is hard to see that, just trust that it will happen. Hang in there."

Gabrielle is certainly proof of that. With determination and perseverance, Gabby hung in there to get where she is today. It's a positive cycle she plans to continue for a long time to come.

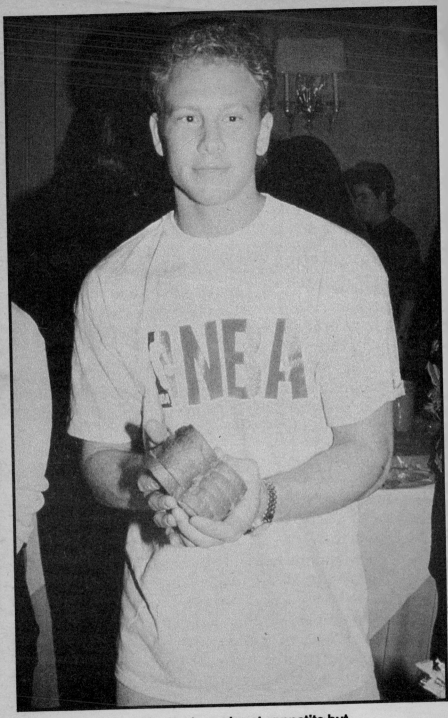

Ian Ziering has a hearty appetite but
working out keeps this hunk in super shape.

CHAPTER 5

Ian Ziering Plays Steve Sanders

The Z-Man is nothing like his character Steve Sanders. Ian is outgoing, cheerful, confident, and thoughtful of others. He is not spoiled, selfish, or insecure like Steve. But he's such a good actor, people who meet him are often surprised at how warm and wonderful he is!

Ian Ziering was born in West Orange, New Jersey to parents Paul and Mickie on March 30th, twenty-something years ago. He has two older brothers, Jeffrey and Barry, both businessmen in New Jersey.

This blond-haired, blue-eyed babe got his start in acting at the tender age of 12. His first movie role was in *Endless Love* as Brooke Shields's younger brother. Ian made his Broadway debut in *I Remember Mama*.

Ian attributes his success to persistence and dedication. "You've got to be a threat to the competition. It's a cutthroat business and you need to be sharper than anyone else around." That's why Ian also took singing and dance lessons. He wanted to know that if a part came up where those skills were needed, he could handle it.

After high school graduation Ian won the role of Cameron Stewart on the afternoon soap opera, *The Guiding Light.* This lasted nearly three years. But Ian was also determined to continue with his education and attended William Paterson College in New Jersey where he received a degree in theater arts. The Z-Man is one cool dude!

When Ian's contract ran out on *The Guiding Light,* this fair-haired guy once again made his round of auditions, all of which he took very seriously. "I treat each audition as if it were gold. I try to make every one count." Finally, after a full year of trying very hard, Ian's *Beverly Hills, 90210* audition counted...big! After only two tryouts, Ian made the final cut and won the role of Steve Sanders.

Then it was off to Hollywood. Although Ian found if difficult to adjust to the west coast at first, he now feels comfortable there. He has a pet dog named Coty and has become close with his *90210* castmates. In his free time—what little he has—Ian likes to go swimming, diving, or skiing. He's very athletic and plays all sports, but his faves are soccer, baseball, and basketball.

The Z-Man's other interests include collecting fish. He has a 55 gallon saltwater fish tank in his LA apartment and an even bigger one at home in New Jersey. Ian is also actively involved in charity work and helping the elderly. "It's unfortunate that we really don't have a viable way for the elderly to get elderly comfortably," says Ian.

What's in the Z-Man's future? A relationship, of course. Ian has been a little lonesome since he broke up with his high school sweetheart, but *90210* keeps him busy. He also has Coty, and there's certain to be a new honey in Ian's life real soon. Do you know anyone who's interested?

Sweet, sensible Jennie Garth plays
spoiled, selfish Kelly Taylor.

CHAPTER 6

Jennie Garth Plays Kelly Taylor

"I was a tomboy," says Jennie Garth. "We had horse stables on the farm and I grew up taking care of the horses, riding, and roughhousing with my brothers. I helped take care of all the animals." Jennie's just the opposite of her character Kelly Taylor, who grew up amongst the rich and famous in Beverly Hills. But she's so good at her job, that it's hard to believe she isn't the snobby, spoiled girl she portrays.

Jennifer Eve Garth was born on April 3, 1972 to John and Carolyn Garth in Champaign, Illinois. She is the youngest of seven children. She looks back on her childhood with fondness. "Growing up on a farm in such a tight family gave me incredible morals and values. I know it sounds hokey, but I fell like I'm a Walton. There were no traumas. Only the best things stand out when I think back on my childhood."

When Jennie was 13 her family had to sell the farm and move to Arizona on account of her father's health. "We needed to be in a warmer, dryer climate," she explains. While at first Jennie had difficulty adjusting to city life in Phoenix, it was there that she got her first taste of the show biz world. "Phoenix was where I got into dance more seriously. I started taking lessons every Saturday and became really devoted to it," says Jennie.

Although Jennie was focused only on her dancing career, her coaches and trainers told her she should try modeling and enter talent contests. Jennie took their advice, and that's when she was discovered. "I was spotted by a Hollywood talent manager, but it wasn't quite as simple or as fast as all that," says Jennie. "I had to put in a lot of work before I really became an actress."

After four years of very hard work—acting lessons, voice lessons, and more—Jennie was ready to go to Hollywood. At age 17 she and her mom moved to LA to work with Jennie's manager Randy James. Her dad stayed home to take care of her siblings and they both really missed him. But Jennie began winning roles almost as soon as she got to California. She was cast in *Teen Angel Returns* where she first met Jason Priestley. Next came an episode of *Growing Pains*. Then she co-starred in the short-lived series, *A Brand New Life*.

Jennie had to audition five times to win the role of Kelly on *90210*. She beat out several hundred competitors. But now that she's part of the *Beverly Hills* family, Jennie can relax a little and enjoy her role. She can also enjoy her new friendships with her castmates.

Always thoughtful, Jennie has endeared herself to practically everyone on the set. She brings in homemade goodies and crochets little dolls as presents. Luke Perry describes Jennie as "sweetness" and claims that they are soulmates because they are both farm people.

Although Jennie now lives in a brand new home in Los Angeles, being a country girl is still a part of her life. She makes frequent trips back home to see her family and tries to do things outdoors as often as possible. With Jennie's popularity though, that's becoming harder and harder. Still, her idea of an ideal date is to take her best beau and her dog Sasha on a picnic in the park. These days she's doing just that with handsome honey Dan Clark. You may be hearing more about him in the future, but you can be sure you'll be seeing and hearing more about Jennie Garth for many years to come!

**Show biz kid Brian Green
plays David "DJ" Silver, the class clown.**

CHAPTER 7

Brian Green Plays David Silver

On screen, David Silver is now a sophomore, is going steady with Donna, and is finally being accepted by the "in-crowd." Off screen, Brian Green has turned 18, has bought his own home, and is "stretching his wings" as an independent, responsible guy. However, while David Silver still struggles to maintain his spot in the limelight, Brian Green has been a shining star for many years.

Born July 15, 1973 in Van Nuys, California, Brian has been a part of the show biz world since he was born. Brian's dad George is a professional drummer whose beat can be heard on such shows as *The Simpsons*. It came as no surprise when Brian seemed to have inherited his father's talents. Brian says his first ambition was, "to be a drummer like my dad." To help foster this, Bri's parents enrolled their talented boy in a special school for gifted children in the performing arts.

In the third grade, however, Brian was bitten by the acting bug. He was asked to act in some films being made by local university students, and he took to his first acting experience like a fish to water. Soon Brian was winning roles in TV shows and commercials on a regular basis. At the ripe old age of 10, Brian was cast in the drama series, *Knot's Landing.* His role of Brian Cunningham lasted four years.

Throughout his *Knots Landing* stint, Brian was tutored on the set, but after his role ended, he attended North Hollywood High School which he graduated from in June, 1991.

The year before he graduated though, was another banner year for Brian. It was the year he won the role of David Silver on *Beverly Hills, 90210.* Brian was thrilled to be a part of this fabulous show. "I'd seen so many scripts about teens that I couldn't relate to at all. Here was one that I finally could. So I worked extra hard on the audition. I really wanted this part."

And what a plum role it's been. Brian has been able to help his character grow and he himself has matured at the same time. "David's come a long way since the beginning of the series, and I hope I have, too."

In fact, Brian seems to keep growing up right in front of our eyes. He now lives alone, and while he admits that at first it was scary, he's gotten used to it. The Green Man is also spending time cultivating his other interests. Brian's never given up his love of music—he's the best hip-hop rap dancer on the set —and he's formed a group "Think Twice" with best pal Robin Thicke, son of *Growing Pains* Alan Thicke. The group hopes to release an album real soon.

Brian's also involved in charity and is a self-proclaimed animal lover. It's a rare weekend that he doesn't make a personal appearance to help a cause like Cystic Fibrosis for Athletes, The Starlight Foundation, or Entertainers for Kids.

With his busy schedule, Brian hardly has time for a social life. In what little spare time he has, however, Brian likes to dance, sing, surf, skateboard, and ski. As to the girls in Brian's life? There's no one special right now, but Brian's always on the lookout. He says in that respect, he's like his character David. "I really like all kinds of girls—I just like girls!" And from the amount of fan mail Brian receives, they like him, too!

Beautiful Tori Spelling vamps for the cameras.

CHAPTER 8

Tori Spelling Plays Donna Martin

Tori Spelling may be the most misunderstood cast member. She is rich, attractive, bright, and talented. She lives in a mansion, has a BMW, several portable phones, a movie theater in her house, and gets invited to the best parties. But, unlike many of her "schoolmates" at West Beverly High, Tori Spelling is not spoiled, stuck-up, ditzy, or unapproachable. In fact, she's just the opposite.

Although Victoria Davey Spelling was born into the lap of luxury on May 16, 1973, she's always been a sweet, sensitive, and caring person. However, she does admit that growing up as the daughter of famous producer Aaron Spelling has been fun. "When I was younger, my dad always took me to cast parties and affairs. I would meet the stars and it got me used to being around those types of people. So it was easier for me to break into the business and be more comfortable with it."

However, when Tori decided she wanted to be an actress, she was determined to do it on her own. "My mom and dad never pushed me," says Tori. "It was more a case of they wanted for me what I wanted for me." Tori took drama lessons in school and later with a private instructor. Her first roles were in school plays.

While Tori's early professional roles were bit parts on some of her dad's shows like *T.J. Hooker* and *Hotel*, Tori made her movie debut in *Troop Beverly Hills*, a flick that was not an Aaron Spelling production. This gave Tori the confidence to continue acting and when she tried out for a role in *Beverly Hills, 90210* it was without her father's knowledge. While Tori had hopes of playing Kelly Taylor, she was cast as Donna Martin, instead. Tori was thrilled to be part of this cool show in any role and has brought more depth and humor to her character.

When asked what the differences and similarities between herself and Donna Martin are, Tori says, "She makes fun of people who aren't popular, but I'm not like that. She's into her appearance, and she doesn't care about school. I think I'm different from her in all those aspects. But we're both funny!"

Tori's *90210* castmates agree. "She has the wildest, most bizarre, driest sense of humor I've ever come across!" says best pal Shannen Doherty. One-time date Luke Perry agrees. "She's got a great sense of humor!"

Tori has also been credited with being everyone's friend, a trait she holds close to her heart. "I try to always be there for my friends, whenever they need me," says Tori. "She's a very objective person and I like that," says Shannen.

In her spare time, Tori loves shopping, "After all it's my life," she jokes, as well as tennis, volleyball, and painting. Tori is also a talented writer whose future goals include screenwriting and directing. Who knows, maybe someday Tori may take a shot at producing. You know, it's in her genes!

Stunning
Shannen Doherty
is all dressed up
for a night on the town
with handsome fiancé
Chris Foufas.

Jennie Garth
with best beau
Dan Clark at
the *90210*
Mattel dolls
unveiling.

CHAPTER 9

Gossip, Gossip, Gossip

They're so hot, they're so cool, they're so hip, everybody wants to know **everything** about them. It's hard to keep up with the *90210* superstars, but here's the latest line on these Beverly Hills hipsters. Check it out!

THE JUICE ON JASON

The word's out that this blue-eyed babe is going to make his mark on the silver screen. Jay is going to star in the movies. He's in the final contractual stages with Columbia Pictures for the film *Me & Monroe*. Set in the 1950s, Jay will play a teenager who goes to Hollywood to meet the legendary Marilyn Monroe. Should all go well, Jay's set to shoot this film during *90210's* spring break!

But that's not all. Jay has a second deal with Columbia that allows him to produce, direct, or star in any picture he wants to. Wow! Is that superstardom, or what?

As to the Jaybird's personal life, things are happening there as well. Jason took Christine Elise with him on a house-hunting expedition. The two have been dating for several months ever since Christine played Emily Valentine on *90210*. Is this to be a joint purchase? Only time will tell.

THE LOAD ON LUKE

Luke bared all—well only his hunky chest—at a fund-raiser for AIDS. While Luke blushed a bit, a glance at this guy's perfect pecs raised the price of the T-shirt he was wearing to $2000!

But wait, there's more! Rumor has it that Madonna has a crush on Luke. When she was given an award for her participation in raising money for AIDS research she asked none other than Coy Luther to present it to her. Luke was happy to do the honors, but denies any claims that he and the Material Girl are dating. However, did you know that Luke **does** have a crush on Linda Hamilton from *The Terminator* flicks. Wait till Arnold finds out!

You'll be happy to hear that you'll be seeing more of Luke on the big screen. He's signed a two movie deal with 20th Century Fox. Here's looking at you, kid!

THE SCOOP ON SHANNEN

Sensational Shannen became engaged to 25-year-old honey Chris Foufas. Off the set these days, she's sporting a 6 1/2 carat diamond ring. Unfortunately, Chris lives in Chicago. Everyone thinks Chris is a sweetie. Shannen of course knows that, but friends say she should wait a while before tieing the knot. Who knows if Shannen will take their advice? Although the couple haven't set a date yet, rumor has it the wedding will take place sometime this year!

THE GAB ON GABRIELLE

Congrats are also in order for this lovely lady. She and honey Charlie Issacs are planning to tie the knot, too! These two sweethearts have known each other for some time now, and Charlie's so in love with Gabby that he followed her out to LA when she got cast in *90210*! He proposed in romantic Hawaii and the two plan a spring or summer wedding. Isn't love grand!

THE BEAT ON BRIAN

Catch this! Brian would love to star in a horror movie. He says, "There's nothing better than being packed full of fake blood and exploding on screen in front of hundreds of people. Yeah. I'd love to do something that gross!" Brian might love it, but it's probably not the best way for him to meet girls. What do you think?

If that's not enough, Brian's also into weird pets. Rumor has it that he's about to buy a ferret and he's going to call him Spike! Brian's also been known to say that if he could come back as an animal, he'd be an eagle. He likes birds of prey! Sounds like an **interesting** kind of guy!

THE JIVE ON JENNIE GARTH

Did you hear? This beautiful, blond-haired, blue-eyed gal showed up with a beautiful, blond-haired, blue-eyed guy at Mattel's kickoff celebration for the new, and certain to be bigger than Barbie, *90210* dolls. But no, this guy is not Jennie's brother, he's her best beau. Some rumors even say that these two hand-holders are engaged. Well, there isn't any ice flashing on Jennie's hand, yet, but who knows, it seems as if the *Beverly Hills* gals are headed down the aisle!

THE TRUTH ABOUT TORI

Although Tori Spelling is one of the few real Beverly Hills hipsters having grown up in a mansion in Bel Air, if truth be told, she is not a snob. Tori confides that there was pressure to be popular in her high school, like on the show, but in real life she wasn't obsessed with the "in-crowd." Tori says, "It's not important to me where my friends come from or how much money they have. I'm friends with lots of different people with different backgrounds and interests!" Good for you, Tori!

ALL EYES ON IAN

The six foot, 175 pound Z-Man is quiet the strapping hunk, and very athletic, too. However, he's not completely at home on the tennis court. The word traveling through the grapevine is that when Ian played in a celebrity tennis tournament recently, he accidentally smashed his tennis partner, designer Mary McFadden, in the side. She suffered two broken ribs! He must have a powerful serve, but maybe Ian should stick to singles!

THE BEST ON BEVERLY HILLS, 90210

Get out the milk! Chances are you'll soon be eating a cereal based on the show! While negotiations are still underway, it's a safe bet there will be a snap, crackle, and pop to the West Beverly beat.

And if that's not enough, rumor has it that both Pepsi and Coca-Cola want the *90210* hipsters to appear in their commercials. What's next, *90210* frozen foods?

Jason Priestley and
Northern Exposure's **Janine Turner make a nice couple, but Christine Elise is Jay's steady gal.**

Fiancé Charlie Issacs bestows a flower upon his lovely Gabrielle.

CHAPTER 10

Quotable Quotes— The Last Word

Hey, do you know what they say? Those babes on Beverly Hills speak up! Listen closely now!

Shannen Doherty on Shannen Doherty

"I am not the type of girl who runs around with everyone I meet. I watch what people do, how they act, and what they are like first. I want to get to know someone first before becoming fast friends."

Shannen Doherty on Acting

"I don't worry about my work. I worry about doing good work. I feel pressure everyday to put out quality stuff."

Jason Priestley on Being an Actor

"I guess a lot of people get into acting because they want the fame and glamorous lifestyle, but that was not my intention at all. I just love to act!"

Beverly Hills, 90210 dolls from Mattel. Move over Barbie!

It's something I've been doing ever since I was a little kid."

Jason Priestley on the Big Apple
"The one thing I like about New York is that a lot of people walk to where they want to go. In Los Angeles, people will think you're a freak if you tell them you're walking to the grocery store."

Tori Spelling on Donna Martin
"My look is really kind of different from Donna's. She dresses up much more than I do. I'm into looking casual, wearing more comfy clothes like jeans and T-shirts."

Tori Spelling on Fame
"I can't believe how big *Beverly Hills, 90210* is right now. Everywhere I go I see T-shirts and posters on sale and hear people screaming, 'Donna! Donna!' It's a little weird."

Luke Perry on Thrills
"I love it when there's constant excitement in my life and the challenge of doing things that scare me!"

Luke Perry on Responsibility
"I truly believe that my generation has the responsibility and capability to enact the necessary changes to make the world a better place."

Brian Green on Gabrielle Carteris
"Gabrielle is such a great listener. We all come to her with our problems."

Brian Green on the Sideburn Solution
"There are old pictures of Jason with long sideburns and there are old pictures of Luke, and he didn't have sideburns."

Gabrielle Carteris on Kissing
"Whenever I have to kiss someone such as Jason Priestley, I usually introduce my boyfriend (now fiancé) to the one I'm doing the scene with. Then I have fun. I go for it."

Gabrielle Carteris on Ian Ziering
"I know that no matter what, Ian will always be there for me if I need him."

Ian Ziering on Fans
"I always read my fan mail, especially during downtime and anytime there's a phone number, I'll always call and say, 'Hey thanks for writing the letter and while I might not be able to write back real soon, I did get your letter and I really appreciate it.'"

Ian Ziering on Success
"Right now I'm just riding the wave and very thankful for what's happening to me."

Jennie Garth on *90210*

"I'm proud to be on this show. It teaches kids that you don't have to be perfect and that's its okay to make mistakes and that you don't have to grow up too quickly."

Jennie Garth on Family

"Living in a small town and coming from a very tight and close family instilled a lot of standards that I need to live up to."

**All decked out are
Brian Green, Jennie Garth, Tori Spelling and
their handsome honeys.**

Luke Perry and Jason Priestley with buddy Charlie Sheen.

CHAPTER 11

The *Beverly Hills, 90210* Trivia Quiz

How much do you know about TV's top teen show and its stars? Test your *Beverly Hills* IQ with the following quiz.

1.) In what state does Dylan McKay's mother live?
2.) Who's older, Brandon or Brenda?
3.) What is Steve's mom's profession?
4.) What does David's dad do?
5.) From what part of California is Andrea?
6.) Who does Andrea live with while attending West Beverly High?
7.) What did Donna dress up as in the 1991 Halloween episode?
8.) Who visited the Walshes home on Christmas Eve 1991?
9.) How did Brandon's cousin get injured?
10.) Who is Kelly's mother planning to marry?

**Shannen Doherty, Ian Ziering, and Jennie Garth
have a blast in London!**

MULTIPLE CHOICE

11.) Jason's first commercial was at the age of
a) 5 years b) 6 months c) 2 years

12.) Tori Spelling's father was the producer of
a) *Dallas* b) *Happy Days* c) *Dynasty*

13.) Gabrielle Carteris originally wanted to be a
a) teacher b) dancer c) doctor

14.) Ian Ziering owns a pet
a) ferret b) pig c) dog

15.) Shannen was most influenced by actor
a) Michael Landon b) Steve Martin c) Jason Priestley

16.) Brian starred as a child in the series
a) *Leave it to Beaver* b) *Knots Landing* c) *Little House on the Prairie*

17.) Luke Perry used to be a (N)
a) construction worker b) mailman c) acrobat

18.) Gabrielle Carteris is engaged to a(n)
a) actor b) producer c) stockbroker

19.) Shannen's fiancé hails from the city of
a) New York b) Chicago c) California

20.) Tori's least favorite subjects in school were
a) english and spanish b) math and physics c) history and french

TRUE OR FALSE

21.) Brandon had a "fatal attraction" romance with Emily Valentine? ___T ___F

22.) Steve still has a thing for Kelly? ___T___F

23.) Brenda was interested in a guy she met at aerobics class.___T___F

24.) Donna is going out with a younger guy. ___T___F

25.) Kelly's mom and Donna's dad are an item.___T___F

26.) Brandon and Brenda's parents are divorced.___T___F

27.) Brandon fell for an aspiring Olympic skater. ___T___F

28.) Luke took Brenda to give blood on Valentine's Day 1992.___T___F

29.) Andrea still has a crush on Luke.___T___F

30.) Brandon and Andrea went to the 1991 spring dance together. ___T___F

FILL IN THE BLANKS

31.) Jason Priestley hails from _____, British Columbia.

32.) Shannen Doherty's fiancé lives in _____, IL.

33.) Tori Spelling grew up in a mansion in _____, CA.

34.) Ian Ziering is originally from _____, NJ.

35.) Gabrielle Carteris's fiancé followed her to LA from _____ city.

36.) Luke Perry grew up in Fredericktown, _____.

37.) Jennie Garth was born in Champaign, _____.

38.) Brian Green is a native of Van Nuys, _____.

39.) Gabrielle Carteris was born in Phoenix, _____.

40.) Shannen Doherty is originally from _____, Tennessee.

ANSWERS TO TRIVIA:

1. Hawaii; 2. Brandon; 3. actress; 4. dentist; 5. the San Fernando Valley; 6. her grandmother; 7. a mermaid; 8. Santa Claus; 9. skiing accident; 10. David's dad; 11. a; 12. c; 13. b; 14. c; 15. a; 16. b; 17. a; 18. c; 19. b; 20. b; 21. T; 22. T; 23. T; 24. T; 25. F; 26. F; 27. T; 28. T; 29. F; 30. T; 31. Vancouver; 32. Chicago; 33. Bel Air; 34. West Orange; 35. New York; 36. Ohio; 37. Illinois; 38. California; 39. Arizona; 40. Memphis.

Pals Shannon, Ian, Gabrielle, and Jason hang out together.

CHAPTER 12

Personalized Puzzles

JASON'S JUMBLE

Jason has mixed up the following words. Unscramble them and see if you can figure out what he's trying to tell you!

KEUL, BRLGELIAE, NIA, NBIRA, ESNNAHN, RIOT, IJNENE, NDA EM TNAW UOY OT YSATDE NDTUE OT RUO WHOS. EB REHTE!

Answers on Page 64

GET SCRAMBLING WITH GABRIELLE

Unscramble the words below to find out more about Gabby's character, Andrea Zuckerman.

YIANBR _ _ _ _ _ _
DRETOI _ _ _ _ _ _
GNLSIE _ _ _ _ _ _
TYETPR _ _ _ _ _ _
GTOUOIGN _ _ _ _ _ _ _ _
TPTIEE _ _ _ _ _ _

SHANNEN'S WORD SEARCH

Can you find the following words that have to do with Shannen's character, Brenda Walsh, in the puzzle below? Look up, down, backward, forward, and diagonally.

Caring
Smart
Pretty
Dylan
Brandon
Confident
Twin
Friend

Answers on Page 64

LUKE PERRY'S ZIG ZAG

Luke has hidden the names of the 90210 characters in this puzzle. Look closely now. The names twist in all directions.

Brandon
Brenda
Dylan
Steve
David
Donna
Kelly
Andrea

A	N	D	X	S	M	T	S	L
V	B	R	O	A	B	E	V	X
Z	N	E	A	D	P	V	Q	R
D	D	P	L	N	B	A	E	S
E	A	V	R	E	D	O	N	Q
V	H	B	I	O	Y	V	X	N
I	G	N	O	D	M	L	L	Y
J	W	N	V	X	E	U	A	N
T	B	A	P	K	S	T	W	X

Answers on Page 64

JENNIE'S CROSSWORD

Jennie's crossword is all about her character Kelly. Do you know everything there is to know about the beautiful Beverly Hill's gal?

Across
2. Who does Kelly live with?
4. What classmate did Kelly used to date?
6. Who is Kelly's best friend?
8. Kelly's mom is dating Mr. _____.

Down
1. What color is Kelly's hair?
3. Who is Kelly's other best friend?
5. What is Kelly's last name?
7. What color are Kelly's eyes?

Answers on Page 64

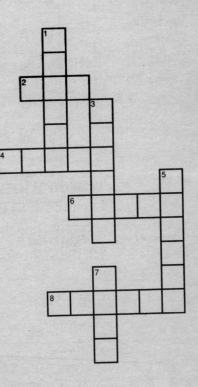

THE Z-MAN'S SEARCH

Can you find the following words that best describe Ian's character, Steve Sanders, in the puzzle below? Look up, down, forward, backward, and diagonally.

Jock
Rich
Spoiled
Smile
Selfish
Handsome
Strong
Cute
Naive

E	P	S	U	O	M	S	D	X	W
M	J	T	Y	L	T	E	E	G	H
O	O	B	R	R	L	A	L	J	E
S	C	I	O	I	H	C	I	R	V
D	K	N	O	G	V	X	M	G	I
N	G	P	R	T	G	X	S	Y	A
A	S	E	L	F	I	S	H	B	N
H	Z	O	G	E	T	U	C	X	A

Answers on page 64

TORI'S HIDDEN MESSAGE

Use the chart below to decode a special message from Tori's character Donna Martin to you.

9-12-12   13-5-5-20   25-15-21   1-20   20-8-5
13-1-12-12!

1	2	3	4	5	6	7	8	9	10	11	12	13	14	15	16
A	B	C	D	E	F	G	H	I	J	K	L	M	N	O	P

17	18	19	20	21	22	23	24	25	26
Q	R	S	T	U	V	W	X	Y	Z

BRIAN'S BEST ON DAVID SILVER

Do you know all there is to know about David "DJ" Silver? If so, try to complete the crossword puzzle below.

Across
3. What does David's dad do?
4. David is a disc _____.
7. Who does David date?
8. What did David buy Donna for her birthday in 1991?

Down
1. David's dad dates _____ mom.
2. David lives in Beverly _____.
5. David is the class _____.
6. David wears an _____ in his ear.

Answers on Page 64

BRIAN'S BEST ON DAVID SILVER

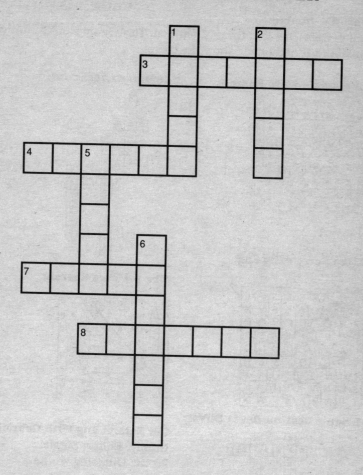

Answers to Puzzles:

Jason's Jumble:
Luke, Gabrielle, Ian, Brian, Shannen, Tori, Jennie and I want you to stayed tuned to our show. Be there!

Shannen's Word Search:

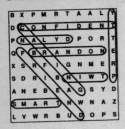

Jennie's Crossword:

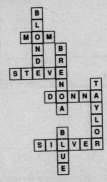

Luke Perry's Zig Zag:

The Z-Man's Search:

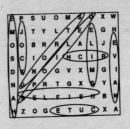

Brian's Best on David Silver:

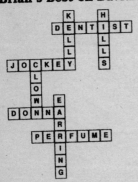

Get Scrambling With Gabrielle:
Brainy; Editor; Single;
Pretty; Outgoing; Petite.

Tori's Hidden Message:
I'll meet you at the mall!